Contents

KT-163-268

Meet the dogs

There are hundreds of different kinds of dogs. This photo shows a basset hound, a golden retriever and a tiny chihuahua.

Newborn   6 weeks   2 months

Life Cycle of a

Dog

Angela Royston

For more information about Heinemann Library books, or to order, please telephone +44 (0)1865 888066, or send a fax to +44 (0)1865 314091. You can visit our web site at www.heinemann.co.uk

First published in Great Britain by Heinemann Library,
Halley Court, Jordan Hill, Oxford OX2 8EJ
a division of Reed Educational and Professional Publishing Ltd.
Heinemann is a registered trademark of Reed Educational & Professional Publishing Ltd.

OXFORD   MELBOURNE   AUCKLAND
JOHANNESBURG   BLANTYRE   GABORONE
IBADAN   PORTSMOUTH (NH) USA   CHICAGO

Designed by Celia Floyd
Illustrated by Alan Fraser
Printed in China by South China Printing Co. Ltd.

05 04 03 02 01
10 9 8 7 6 5 4 3 2 1

ISBN 0 431 08393 2
This title is also available in a hardback library edition (ISBN 0 431 08388 6).

British Library Cataloguing in Publication Data

Royston, Angela
  Life cycle of a dog
  1. Dogs – Life cycles – Juvenile literature
  I. Title II. Dog
  599.7'72

Acknowledgements

The Publisher would like to thank the following for permission to reproduce photographs:

Ardea London: John Daniels p.7, p.8, p.9, p.10, p.20, p.21, p.22, p.24, p.26; FLPA: BS Turner p.17, David Hosking p.18, p.19, Foto Natura p.25, Gerard Lacz p.23, HD Brandl p.16, J&P Wegner p.5, Roger Wilmshurst p.27; John Daniels: p.11, p.15; Marc Henrie Asc. London: p.6, p.12, p.13, p.14; Tony Stone: Tim Davis p.4.

Cover photograph reproduced with the permission of Bruce Coleman.

Every effort has been made to contact copyright holders of any material reproduced in this book. Any omissions will be rectified in subsequent printings if notice is given to the Publisher.

This book tells you about the life of a **female** golden retriever. She has floppy ears and a long tail. She began life as a tiny puppy.

1 year

3 years

8 years

Newborn

The mother dog has given birth to a **litter**. The little **female** puppy is the last to be born. She has lots of brothers and sisters.

Newborn

6 weeks

2 months

Now the **newborn** puppy is clean and dry. She cannot see or hear but she can feel and smell. She smells her mother and the other puppies in the litter.

1 year

3 years

8 years

1 week

The puppy feeds on her mother's milk. She has to push her way through her brothers and sisters to find a **teat** to suckle from.

Newborn   6 weeks   2 months

The puppies feed and grow bigger.
They still cannot stand but they
snuggle up together and sleep.

I year

3 years

8 years

6 weeks

The puppy's eyes have opened and she can see and hear. Her legs are strong now and she plays and explores.

Newborn

6 weeks

2 months

She plays with her brothers and sisters. Sometimes she pretends to fight with one of them. In this way the puppies learn who is stronger.

2 months

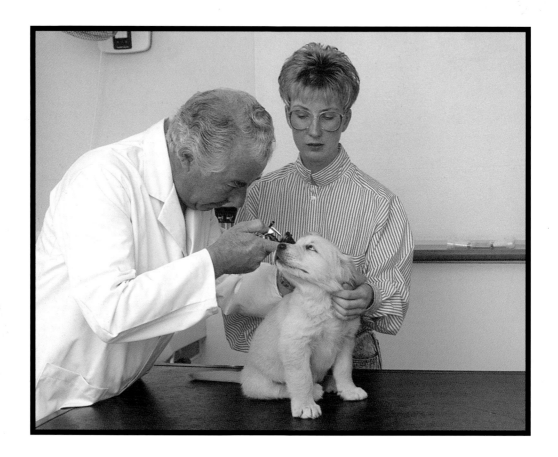

The **vet** examines the puppy all over and gives her a special **injection**. The injection will protect her from catching illnesses.

Newborn   6 weeks   2 months

The puppy can now go outside for the first time. Everything is strange. She has a good sense of smell and uses it to explore.

1 year

3 years

8 years

3 months

The dog leaves her mother and goes to a new owner. She begins to eat solid food now instead of milk. It contains meat and biscuit.

Newborn   6 weeks   2 months

The food gives her **energy** and keeps her healthy. Exercise makes her muscles stronger. She plays with other dogs she meets outside.

1 year

3 years

8 years

1 year

The dog is now fully grown. She has lots of **energy**. When her owner throws a stick, she runs and brings it back.

Newborn 6 weeks 2 months

The word 'retrieve' means to bring back. Retrievers can be **trained** to do tasks and help people. Some are specially trained to be **guide dogs**.

1 year

3 years

8 years

3 months later

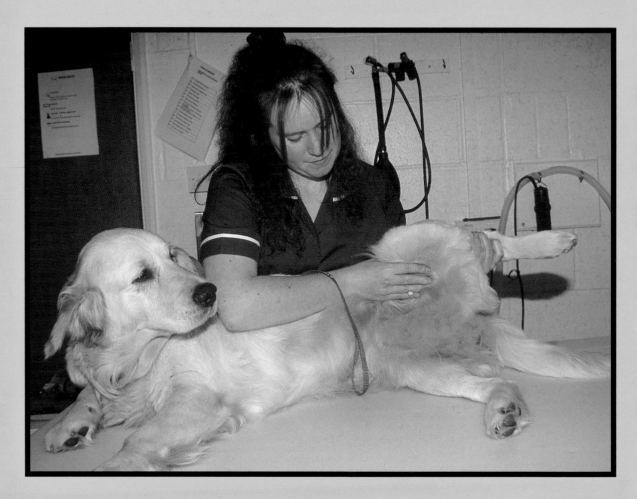

It is time for the dog to go to the **vet** again. The vet takes her pulse and makes sure that she is healthy.

Newborn   6 weeks

2 months

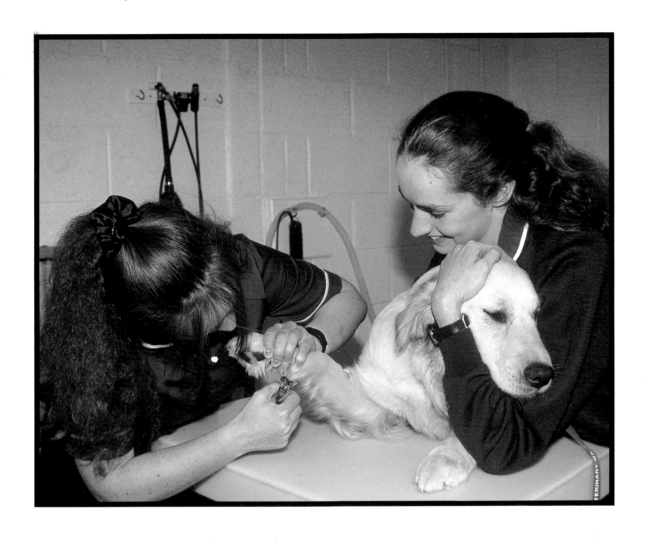

Then she gives the dog a **booster injection** to stop her picking up illnesses. The vet also clips her nails so they do not get too long.

1 year

3 years

8 years

3 years

The dog's owner wants her to have puppies of her own. She is taken to meet a **male** dog and they **mate**.

Newborn   6 weeks   2 months

Now several new puppies are growing inside her. Look how big her stomach is! She is almost ready to give birth.

1 year

3 years

8 years

9 weeks after mating

She gives birth to her **litter** of puppies one by one. The puppies are very small. They feed on her milk and grow quickly.

Newborn   6 weeks   2 months

By the time they are three weeks old they can bark and wag their tails. At nine weeks old the puppies are ready to go to new owners.

1 year   3 years   8 years

5 years

The dog misses her puppies for a few days, but then she forgets about them. She goes back to her old life with her owners.

Newborn   6 weeks   2 months

They take her for long walks.
When they throw a stick she runs
after it. She swims through the
water to fetch the stick.

1 year

3 years

8 years

It's a dog's life

The dog is eight years old now. She still needs exercise every day, but she walks more slowly now and does not run about as before.

Newborn  6 weeks 2 months

Most dogs live until they are ten to
fifteen years old. Small dogs often
live longer than bigger dogs.

1 year

3 years

8 years

Life cycle

Newborn

6 weeks old

2 months old

1 year old

3 years old

8 years old

Fact file

Dogs are a popular pet. There are about 50 million dogs in the United States.

A retriever's hairy coat is **waterproof** so they like being in water.

A dog has such a good sense of smell, it can smell and track a person from the footprints left by their shoes.

Retrievers can have several **litters**. In each litter they usually have seven to nine puppies.

Glossary

booster   a second injection to make the first injection work better

energy   the ability to run around and do things

female   girl

guide dog   a dog which is trained to help blind people find their way round

injection   squirting special liquids into the body to help prevent a particular illness

litter   several baby animals born together

male   boy

mate   when a male and female come together to produce babies

teat   female's nipples through which the puppies suck milk

trained   taught

vet   animal doctor

waterproof   something which keeps out water

Index